Handbook

Susan Tayfoor

ℛ
RAVETTE PUBLISHING

Printed and bound in Great Britain
for Ravette Publishing Limited,
Unit 3, Tristar Centre,
Star Road, Partridge Green,
West Sussex RH13 8RA
by CPD Wales, Ebbw Vale

ISBN: 1 84161 050 X

If someone sees things differently to us,
that doesn't make us right
and them wrong.
They have their truth, we have ours.
There is no black or white,
only shades of grey.

Be Yourself!

Admitting your faults may sound like a weakness,
but instead, it can leave you feeling strong -
giving you the freedom to be who you are
with no image to live up to.

If you try to cover up your faults,
people will sense that you are hiding something.
If you admit to them,
people will admire you for your honesty
and will begin communicating with you
on a more sincere level.

We create our own emotions

Anger, fear or heartbreak
aren't caused by what happens to us,
but from our reactions to what happens.
We create our future
from the way we respond to our present.

If someone angers or annoys you,
they can only do so if you let them,
by choosing to feel anger or pain.
Why feel bad for the rest of the day,
or even longer?
It's your mind, you decide
what thoughts to fill it with.

Once you let go of a bad feeling,
that space can then be filled with a new energy.

We can't prevent negative thoughts
from coming into our mind,
but there's no need to invite them
to sit down and make themselves at home.

It's your mind.
Choose to fill it
with images of beauty
and inspiration.

Learning from our mistakes

However many times life knocks you down,
get up and keep on walking.
When the way ahead is blocked,
instead of sitting down and giving up,
you can simply change direction.

Nothing happens accidentally.
Events and people come into your life because
you attracted them there
to learn from.

When we are ready to learn,
we will discover that the answer
was there all along.

It's all a Question of Perspective

'The world is a looking glass
and gives back to every man
the reflection of his own face,'
wrote Thackeray.

The world lives up to our expectations.
You can find a reality out there
that confirms your inner view of things.
You can often change the world
simply by changing your way of looking at it.

Our perception of the world is formed
from our experience
and is subjective and unique.

If someone sees things differently to us,
that doesn't make us right
and them wrong.
They have their truth, we have ours.
There is no black or white,
only shades of grey.

Leaving others free
to be who they are

Everyone is author of their own story
and must write their own script.
You can offer people your advice,
but you can't force them to take it.

When we have hopes and dreams for someone else,
we give them the power to disappoint or agitate us
if they don't fulfil them.
Let's keep our dreams for ourselves,
regain control of our peace of mind
and leave others free to be who they are.

Learn to measure people as to how
they live up to their own expectations,
rather than criticising them
for failing to live up to yours.

Living our own lives ...
not anyone else's

When we constantly shield someone
from the consequences of their own harmful actions,
we are not allowing them to learn
the lessons they need
in order to grow
and take responsibility for their lives.

You can't blame yourself for someone else's decisions,
or always try to protect them
from the consequences of their actions.
Accept that they have their own path to follow
and you can't walk all the way with them,
holding the map and the umbrella!

The best gift you can give yourself
is your own
wholehearted approval!
Only when you do that, are you free
to live life YOUR way.

Happiness comes when we can look
at the good and bad within ourselves
and accept it as part of the whole,
without judging any right or wrong.

It means not denying or being ashamed of what
you think and feel, but knowing
that you are good enough as you are
and, instead of criticising the parts,
being able to embrace, accept and love the whole.

When we suppress and deny our feelings,
they metamorphose into something different,
hiding themselves more subtly,
transmuting, making our selves more 'complex',
muddying the clear waters of our soul.

Let an emotion ride its course ...
When you feel upset, rather than trying
to hold back the tears,
cry until you're through,
then busy yourself with something else.

Who am 'I'?

'All humanity is one undivided and indivisible
family,' wrote Mohandas Gandhi.
We are all drops of water
floating within the ocean of life.
We just don't always recognise our connection.

When we die, we simply change form,
like a kettle of boiling water
transforms into steam.
Where did the water go?

We can't define ourselves by our possessions,
or by our status, since these things come and go.
Instead, we are defined by the way we think ...
We are who we believe ourselves to be,
since we act according to our thoughts.

Don't place limits on life

Once we define ourselves as being
a particular type of person,
each definition serves merely to
limit us and set our boundaries.
Who says you don't do that sort of thing?

For most of us, the walls that hold us back
exist only in our minds.

These limits are there,
only because we acknowledge them.
Let's try eliminating words like 'should' or 'can't'
from our way of thinking.

Love

Love makes us feel alive and new,
because it releases us from the boundaries
of our 'self'
and makes us reconnect
to the universe around us.

'If you would have all the world love you,
you must first love all the world,'
wrote Ralph W. Twine.
Rather than waiting passively for love,
start being loving in your everyday life.

Giving and receiving love
makes us feel powerful,
since it blocks off our illusion
of 'separateness' from the world.

Making Ourselves Whole ...

When we look for our 'other half',
we are busy seeking from others
what we lack in ourselves.

Rather than trying to find someone
who can give us the strengths
and qualities we lack,
why not try to develop
these qualities in ourselves?

Ultimately, any refuge or shelter we seek,
can only be found within ourselves.

Accepting Others

Learn to love someone for who they are,
without superimposing our expectations onto them,
or seeing them
through the filter of our past experiences
and judging what they say or do accordingly.

There is no 'right' or 'wrong' way of living,
only ways that are different
to ours.

Giving someone unconditional love
means giving them permission to try and fail
and still loving them the same.

Creating our world anew

Letting go of how you think things *should* be,
gives you the freedom to enjoy things
as they truly are,
with a sense of wonder at their 'newness'.

Walk through life accepting it,
rather than resisting anything unexpected.
Take each situation as a fresh one,
acting, instead of re-acting.

Sharpen your senses!
When you eat a strawberry,
does it simply taste of water, or
can you taste the sun, the wind
and the rain inside it?

The secret of living a spiritual life,
is not to see different surroundings,
but learning to see
our surroundings differently.

Accepting what life offers

If we walk through life loaded with expectations
and firm beliefs of how things are
and how others should be,
we'll find plenty of things to disappoint
and anger us along the way.

Once we drop these rules we've made,
we can breeze through life,
feeling calmer and lighter,
being pleasantly surprised every now and then.

Life plays according to its own rules,
not ours ...

Life deals us the cards.
The way we choose to play them
is up to us.

We can strive to change the future,
but we can only accept things as they are
right now.

To spend our life searching for perfection,
means we are trained at spotting
only the flaws in what we already have,
and miss the beauty all around us.

Our Purpose in Life

The main reason we are here,
is to live life and enjoy it,
by being happy ourselves
and making others happy.

Think of life as an enormous ice cream sundae!
Some people eat it with relish,
some sit idly by and watch it melt
and others eat it angrily, complaining that they'd
ordered vanilla and got strawberry!

Wherever you're heading
will be the same as where you are now,
since you carry your world within you.

Sometimes we chase after external goals
as a way of running from
the emptiness inside us …

Making the most of what you have

Do you commute to work?
Use this time constructively.
Quieten your mind, concentrate
on this present moment.

Listen to your inner voice -
see what ideas come to you.

Or spend ten minutes of each day on a hobby.
Take a walkman with you and learn a language.
Time isn't a commodity to be frittered away.
If you have a few minutes here and there,
learn to use them.

Living in a world of flux and change

To find something better,
don't be afraid of letting go.
As André Gide wrote:
'One doesn't discover new lands
without consenting to lose sight
of the shore for a very long time.'

Our life goes in cycles …
We can only live with the winter,
because we know that spring
is just around the corner.

Be willing to accept changes.
'You get tragedy,' wrote Wittgenstein,
'where the tree, instead of bending, breaks.'
Be a reed, not an oak tree!

Making our minds a friendly place

Stop criticising yourself
and just be who you are.

Our worst enemies
are the doubts and fears
that lurk inside our own mind,
growing round our hopes and dreams
like creeping vines,
blocking out the sunlight.

We are enough as we are

When we realise our own approval is all we need,
we stop wasting our energy,
defending our views and explaining our actions
and we can take responsibility for our own life
and live it how we choose!

By accepting ourselves as we are,
we can shrug off others' slights and rudeness
as faults and foibles for them to resolve, not us,
and keep our inner selves unruffled.

Loving ourselves as we are
means we are not afraid to try and fail,
until we finally succeed.
We can be relaxed about the result,
because we know that we are already good enough.

Living Life to the full

'For man the vast marvel is to be alive,'
wrote D. H. Lawrence.
Wake up to the wonder of it!

When you live every day
as though it were your last,
time becomes a precious commodity,
not something to be squandered.
The beauty of life consists of getting full value
from each moment and experiencing
each emotion to the full.

Imagine your life as a garden,
divided into four sections:
emotional, physical, spiritual and intellectual.
You need to tend to all four corners,
to be able to enjoy it fully.

Trying to control life,
is like trying to orchestrate
the sunrise and sunset.

Rather than wasting our energy
trying to control all events in our lives,
to make sure everything runs to plan,
why don't we trust instead, that
the world doesn't need us to run it,
and events will unfold regardless of us.

Let's put our energy instead
into simply making the most
of where we are.

Living Authentically

Why strive after someone else's
definition of success,
when we can create our own?

'Our life is what our thoughts make it,'
wrote Marcus Aurelius.
There's no use searching outside for your destiny.
It lies within you,
with every incipient thought and feeling.

Once we trust ourselves, we are free to act,
instead of holding back
while we ask for everyone else's approval
except our own.

The most important goal in life
is to live authentically.
How?

By taking the time to listen to ourselves,
to the quiet voice inside that prompts us
and lets us know who we really are.

Enlightenment means wakening
to the beauty of the world around you.

Letting go of Anger

When someone close to you annoys you,
instead of dwelling on what they've done,
think of three reasons why you love them,
then picture them,
and feel the anger within you dissolve.

When we forgive others for the hurt they cause us,
it's not so much for their benefit
as for ours.
By letting go of the pain and anger,
we shed the emotions restricting our growth,
like a snake sheds its dead skin.

There's nothing wrong with feeling anger,
so long as we don't bottle it up and store it
'til it turns rancid.

Masks

As we grow up and learn
some feelings are 'unacceptable',
we cover them over with a mask,
so we can present an
acceptable, made-up face to the world,
while we cry underneath.

In time, we come to play a number of roles,
acting in the way that's expected of us,
thirsting for approval from others.

We've worn these masks for so long,
we no longer recognise
our true selves and feelings
beneath them.

Unpeel the masks
to reveal the true 'you'
underneath.
How?

By taking time to be alone, to listen to yourself,
to find out what you truly feel.

The Illusion of Separateness

When we are afraid that we are not good enough,
to protect ourselves from rejection,
we barricade ourselves in
with a show of arrogance, or unfriendliness,
so no one gets close enough to see who we really are,
creating a sense of separation and aloneness,
which was the very thing we had feared.

Only when we lower our own defences,
do we give others the chance
to reach out and touch us
with love.

To be human, is to be one cell,
in the living body
of God.

We are part of the living, breathing universe.
Loving thoughts are all that are needed
to break through our illusion of 'separateness'
and dissolve the barrier.

Meditation

The goal of meditation
is to help us focus on the present,
to keep our thoughts where they belong,
in the pulsating
NOW
of life.

When we sit with empty minds,
without thoughts,
there is no 'self' there, no limits, no boundaries,
no separateness, no here, no there,
no inside, no outside,
no cut-off point
between ourselves and the universe.
We are simply one.

You don't need to be in special surroundings,
you just need to BE 100% where you are.
The place to start your spiritual quest is here.

There's no use putting it off,
waiting for the 'right' time.
Your life will never be
free of troubles, or things to do.
The right time to start is NOW.

To lead a spiritual life,
it is not so important to give up
our material possessions,
as to give up the pre-conceived opinions and beliefs
we hold onto just as tightly.

Mastering your desires and wants
doesn't mean living in an emotional void.
You can feel the same passions,
but without being attached to the outcome,
or getting caught up in the need to control things.

Recognising our Limitations

'If every rub irritates you,'
wrote Rumi
'how will your mirror be polished?'.

When we get impatient or frustrated,
we bump up against our limits.

When someone makes you angry,
their lesson may be to show you
where your limits lie
and to give you the chance to extend
those boundaries.

Listening to Others ...

Trying to see people
through our own expectations of them,
is like trying to see their reflection
in muddy water.

Only when we're still
and can listen with an empty mind,
we can see them as they truly are.

Are you so busy trying to get your
own message across
that you can't hear anyone else's?

Dealing with Setbacks

When a setback occurs,
rather than panicking, or treating it as a disaster,
take a step back and view it as a lesson.
See what you can learn from the situation,
so as to avoid it the next time round.

When something happens,
we never know at the time
it if is good or bad,
until we can look back on it in retrospect.

Maybe this is the time to make
a major change of direction in your life.
Go with it!
Don't dig your heels in and resist.

Getting what we want

If you want to feed a squirrel,
you don't chase after it with the nuts,
you hold them out and wait for it to come to you.
So it is with everything in life …
When we desperately chase something,
it runs away from us.

We're more likely to succeed
when we simply do our best
and don't worry over the outcome.

Do what you can,
then when there's no more to be done,
step back and focus on something else.

Half of getting what we want,
is learning how to ask for it!

Seeing it through ...

Remember,
an idea is like a tiny seed
with a forest of oak trees inside.
Will you plant one and tend to it,
or simply hold it dormant in your hand?
Ideas need ACTING UPON!

Some people think that if they throw out
a few seeds,
the next day the Universe will deliver them
a loaf of freshly sliced bread!

Our Thoughts become Reality ...

If there's something you don't like,
or don't want to happen,
STOP THINKING ABOUT IT!
The more you focus on it, the more real it becomes.

We play best when it's not so
important to us whether we win or lose,
but that we simply give it our best shot.

When we're too focussed
on one particular outcome,
we fail to notice the golden possibilities
in any other.

Life is right here!

This moment is all that you've got.
Whatever you're doing, do it with full awareness,
not with a mind that's busy elsewhere,
replaying past scenes, or making plans for
the future.

Spend your day being AWARE.
Walk, do some yoga,
relax, trust, laugh and let go.
Accept things as they are at this moment.

Whatever you're doing,
focus on it fully!

What we are looking for
is right here.
The trouble is
that we are often somewhere else.

Trust Yourself!

There is no 'right way' to live.
Take everyone's advice
and you'd end up doing nothing.
The only person to truly listen to is yourself.
Learn to start trusting yourself.

It's much better if we make a mistake,
to know it happened because
we did what we thought was right at the time,
not because we did what someone else
thought was right.

How many times do we hold back from
doing something
for fear that we won't be good enough?

Trusting things to work out fine

Do your best, then relax.
Don't worry about the outcome.
Remember, everything in the world
is exactly as it should be right now,
and it cannot be otherwise.

How much heavier our lives are,
when we're attached to outcomes.
Let's just do our best, where we are
and let life take care of the rest.

Attachments

Money or success in themselves
are not harmful.
It is only our attachment to them
that destroys our peace of mind.

Taking life lightly ...

Life is like a bouquet of roses ...
full of transient beauty,
but also full of painful thorns
for those who try to grasp hold of it
too tightly.

Time for Ourselves

We need to have a space for ourselves
that's comfortable and quiet,
where we feel at home and relaxed
and can sit and dream …

How often do we spend our day listening to others,
but don't take a moment
to sit in silence and listen to ourselves?

Our goal is not to find the truth,
but to stop judging things right or wrong.

When we have too much to do,
the first thing we usually give up
is time for ourselves.

The essential time we need,
to spend in quiet relaxation,
while we reflect upon our lives
and put things back into perspective.

Your spiritual quest in life
is simply to learn
to be who you are.

Other titles available @ £2.99 each ...

	ISBN
A Beauty Handbook	1 84161 046 1
A Happiness Handbook	1 84161 047 X
A Relationship Handbook	1 84161 048 8
A Relaxation Handbook	1 84161 049 6
A Wisdom Handbook	1 84161 051 8

available March 2001 ...

A Communication Handbook	1 84161 073 9
A Dating Handbook	1 84161 074 7

available September 2001 ...

A Power-Thinking Handbook	1 84161 075 5
A Motivation Handbook	1 84161 076 3

Ordering ...   Please send a cheque/postal order in £ sterling, made payable to 'Ravette Publishing Ltd' for the cover price of the book(s) and allow the following for postage and packing ...

UK & BFPO   50p for the first book & 30p per book thereafter
Europe & Eire £1.00 for the first book & 50p per book thereafter
rest of the world £1.80 for the first book & 80p per book thereafter

Ravette Publishing Limited
Unit 3, Tristar Centre, Star Road, Partridge Green,
West Sussex RH13 8RA